DISCARD

MAKING YOUR POINT

ROBERT E. DUNBAR

MAKING YOUR POINT

HOW TO SPEAK AND WRITE PERSUASIVELY

FRANKLIN WATTS | 1990
NEW YORK | LONDON | TORONTO | SYDNEY
A LANGUAGE POWER BOOK

Photographs courtesy of:
UPI/Bettmann Newsphotos: pp. 13, 17, 47, 70, 74, 78;
The Bettmann Archives: pp. 25, 26, 32, 45, 66;
Rothco Cartoons: pp. 36 (Punch), 40, 48, 54.

Grateful acknowledgment for permission to reprint material previously published is made to the following: pp. 22, 23: *The New Republic*; pp. 77-79: Putnam Publishing Group; pp. 82, 83: New York Times Company.

Library of Congress Cataloging-in-Publication Data

Dunbar, Robert E.
Making your point: how to speak and write persuasively/Robert E. Dunbar.
    p. cm.—(A Language power book)
Summary: Discusses ways to effectively use elements such as persuasion, meaningful language, and humor in public speaking and writing.
ISBN 0-531-10905-4
1. Public speaking—Juvenile literature. 2. Authorship—Juvenile literature. 3. Persuasion (Rhetoric)—Juvenile literature. 4. Persuasion (Psychology)—Juvenile literature. [1. Public speaking. 2. Authorship. 3. Persuasion (Psychology)] I. Title. II. Series.
PN4121.D9236 1990
808—dc20   89-25088 CIP
                        AC

Copyright © 1990 by Robert E. Dunbar
All rights reserved
Printed in the United States of America
5 4 3 2 1

For Phil and Hop Briggs,
experts both in making a point

ACKNOWLEDGMENT

I am grateful to the following teachers for their generosity in making material available to me: Bonnie Babb, Marilyn J. Heinrich, Katherine A. Pennington, Judith A. Stafford, and William Travers, Jr., of the English Department, and Garret M. Bensen and Walter E. White of the Social Studies Department, Lincoln Academy, Newcastle, Maine.

CONTENTS

CHAPTER ONE
The Power of Persuasion
11

CHAPTER TWO
The Skillful Use of Facts
21

CHAPTER THREE
The Skillful Use of Logic
30

CHAPTER FOUR
The Skillful Use of Language
42

CHAPTER FIVE
Appealing to the Emotions
63

CHAPTER SIX
Humor as Weapon and Reinforcement
76

CHAPTER SEVEN
Researching, Outlining, and Writing:
Blending the Elements to Make Your Point
84

Appendix A: Choosing a Topic
91

Appendix B: Topics for Essays, Reports,
Research Papers, Speeches, and Debates
95

For Further Reading   103

Index   105

MAKING YOUR POINT

THE POWER OF PERSUASION

1

Persuasion can be one of the most important skills you will ever learn. Its usefulness to you in every area of your life as you mature and take your place in society cannot be overstated. Some of the most important decisions in your life will depend on your ability to persuade. It is also an invaluable skill to use in your schoolwork.

For example, it is an essential element in writing essays, reports, and term or research papers. It is also a skill to be mastered for any public speaking experiences you may have, whether in classroom discussions or in programs before school and public groups, as well as in speaking competitions. From time to time you may be called on to make use of your powers of persuasion in informal debates in the classroom or in formal debates as a member of the school's debating team. All of these experiences are tests of your persuasive skills.

MASTERS OF PERSUASION

One of the most remarkable national figures of this century, Martin Luther King, Jr., a black preacher and civil rights activist, through his powers of persuasion led his people and the nation toward the fulfillment of the ideal and promise of full equality under the laws of the land. In marches and demonstrations characterized by nonviolence on the part of the blacks and the whites who supported them, Reverend King won the compassion and support of the majority of Americans through many of his speeches, in particular the speech that highlighted the March on Washington, held on August 28, 1963. In this speech he told an audience of an estimated 250,000 people, who filled the grounds from the Lincoln Memorial to the Washington Monument, and to millions who followed on television:

I have a dream—a dream of the time when the evils of prejudice and segregation will vanish.

His speech had a poetic rhythm that helped produce an emotional response in those who heard it. At one point he put his written speech aside and spoke these words extemporaneously*:

I say to you today, even though we face the difficulties of today and tomorrow, I still have a dream. It is a dream that is deeply rooted in the American dream. I have a dream that one day this nation will rise up, live out the true meaning of its creed: We hold these truths to be self-evident, that all men are created equal.

*Coretta Scott King, in *My Life with Martin Luther King, Jr.* (New York: Holt, Rinehart and Winston, 1969).

Rev. Martin Luther King, Jr., delivering his historic "I Have a Dream" speech in Washington, D.C., in 1963. Dr. King's eloquence helped galvanize the civil rights movement.

I have a dream that one day on the red hills of Georgia the sons of former slaves and the sons of former slaveowners will be able to sit down together at the table of brotherhood. I have a dream that one day even the state of Mississippi, a state sweltering with the heat of oppression, will be transformed into an oasis of freedom and justice.

I have a dream that my four little children one day will live in a nation where they will not be judged by the color of their skin, but by the content of their character.

I have a dream that one day every valley shall be exalted, every hill and mountain shall be made low. The rough places shall be made plain and the crooked places will be made straight. This is the faith that I go back to the South with. With this faith we will be able to hew out of the mountains of despair the stone of hope. With this faith we will be able to work together, to pray together, to struggle together, to go to jail together, to stand up for freedom together, knowing we will be free one day.

This will be the day when all of God's children will be able to sing with new meaning, "Let freedom ring." So let freedom ring from the prodigious hilltops of New Hampshire; let freedom ring from the mighty mountains of New York. But not only that. Let freedom ring from every hill and molehill of Mississippi, from every mountainside.

When we allow freedom to ring from every town and every hamlet, from every state and every city, we will be able to speed up the day when all of God's children, black men and white men, Jews and Gentiles, Protestants and Catholics, will be able to join hands and sing in the words of the old Negro spiritual, "Free at last! Free at last! Great God A-mighty, we are free at last!"

Five years later, in 1968, Reverend King lost his life for the cause of civil rights for blacks when he was assassinated. A tribute to his success is the national holiday held on the third Monday in January each year in his honor.

Many other famous men and women have excelled in the power of persuasion. We need only look at some of the most familiar events in American and recent world history to find outstanding examples. The U.S. Declaration of Independence, written by Thomas Jefferson, is a masterful example of the use of clear and concise language to make a point, as shown in the following excerpt. It was an inspiration for Reverend King as it has been for all Americans. Here are the most famous lines from that document:

We hold these truths to be self-evident, that all men are created equal, that they are endowed by their creator with certain unalienable rights, that among them are Life, Liberty, and the Pursuit of Happiness. That to secure these rights, Governments are instituted among Men, deriving their just powers from the consent of the governed. That whenever any Form of Government becomes destructive of these ends, it is the Right of the People to alter or abolish it, and to institute new Government, laying its foundation on such principles and organizing its powers in such form, as to them shall seem most likely to effect their Safety and Happiness.

WORDS THAT HELPED
SAVE A NATION

Only a few decades after the United States of America became a country in its own right, its very foundations were threatened by the slavery issue. The country might have split into two nations, a North and a South, but for the persuasive words of those who were willing to fight to keep it united. No one did more to accomplish this in written and spoken words than Abraham Lincoln. Two years before he was nominated for president by the new Republican party, he took part in one of history's most famous debates when he opposed Stephen A. Douglas of Illinois in the race for the U.S. Senate. He lost that race, but he captured the imagination and resolve of those who opposed slavery with a statement that became the hallmark of his debates against Douglas:

A house divided against itself cannot stand. I believe this government cannot endure permanently half slave and half free.

These words were repeated often in his speeches and debates with Douglas. Together with carefully structured arguments encompassing all the elements of persuasion, they united the antislavery groups and brought the desired result: the preservation of the union.

"ASK NOT WHAT YOUR COUNTRY CAN DO FOR YOU"

In any presidential campaign in the United States in the latter part of the twentieth century, opposing points of view tug at the popular will over the question of how to correct social problems. One view is that the government should do more by providing more funds and the bureaucracy to expend them. The other point of view is that the government should not be asked to solve problems that the people can solve themselves. When John F. Kennedy was elect-

In his inaugural address in 1961, President John F. Kennedy inspired the nation with the words "Ask not what your country can do for you—ask what you can do for your country."

ed president in 1960, he startled the nation in his inaugural address with this rousing statement:

In the long history of the world, only a few generations have been granted the role of defending freedom in its hour of maximum danger. I do not shrink from this responsibility—I welcome it . . . The energy, the faith, the devotion which we bring to this endeavor will light our country and all who serve it— and the glow from that fire can truly light the world. And so, my fellow Americans: ask not what your country can do for you—ask what you can do for your country.

This persuasive message captured the people's imagination to such a degree that it led directly to one of the longest and most successful volunteer programs in history: the Peace Corps, a U.S.-sponsored international project that sends Americans abroad to fill critical shortages of skilled and semiskilled labor in countries to which they have been invited.

HOW YOU EXPERIENCE THE POWER OF PERSUASION

If you haven't stopped to think about it, you may not realize what an important part persuasion plays in your life now and how important it will continue to be for as long as you live. It affects every aspect of your life. You may believe that most of the decisions you make are yours alone, but they are not. You have been persuaded to make them; sometimes they are unconscious, and sometimes they are conscious.

For example, how much attention do you pay to the ads on television, radio, billboards, posters, and in newspapers and magazines? Perhaps more than you realize. The most successful ads accomplish their purpose—make their point—in very clear, concise language, the result of many days and weeks of deliberation invested to get your attention and to persuade you to take action—buy the product.

The power of persuasion not only dominates the marketplace, it is an essential part of the democratic way of life. Author Wayne C. Minnick* expressed it this way:

The citizen of a democracy is more often the target of persuasion than he is himself a persuader. The brand of soap he buys and the brand of politics he endorses are likely to be decided in an arena of competing persuasion. If he has discovered reliable canons of criticism with which to evaluate the worth of competing claims, he is able to make wise choices. Lacking these canons, he may find himself taken in by the soap-opera huckster or the political demagogue. Finally, the study of persuasion provides men (and women) with skills that help them attain personal goals. Leadership, prestige, influence—all largely depend, in modern democratic society, on a person's ability to make his views felt with enough force to enlist sympathy and support from others.

THE ELEMENTS
OF PERSUASION

In your efforts to make your point, to be persuasive, certain basic elements are involved. The use you make of them depends to some extent on the kind of project you are dealing with. An essay or book report

---

*Wayne C. Minnick, *The Art of Persuasion* (Boston: Houghton Mifflin Company, 1968).

is a much shorter project than a research or term paper. If you are making a speech, there are time limits. The same goes for debate, informal or formal. Whatever the project, you will be working with some or all of the following elements:

    Facts
    Logic
    Language
    Emotion
    Humor

Facts, logic, and language are basic tools of persuasion no matter what your project happens to be—writing, speaking, or debating. Appeal to the emotions is another basic tool and one you will probably use more often than humor. Humor may or may not be appropriate, depending on the kind of project and your approach to it, but it can be a most effective element when used skillfully. In the chapters that follow each of these elements will be discussed in detail.

THE SKILLFUL USE OF FACTS

2

Whatever point of view you take, whether you're using the written or spoken word, you will have to draw on facts to support it. Opinion may be interesting and interestingly expressed, but it counts for nothing unless it is backed up by facts.

The facts you need to support your point of view can be found in material you have read. They can be based on your own personal experiences and on the experiences of others known to you. They can be found in published reports of both government and nongovernment agencies and in articles and books by respected authorities.

How far you will want to search for facts will depend on your assignment. For instance, in a book report your assignment is to discuss the book. All the facts you need to support your point of view may be there. No research may be necessary unless the book is controversial and you do not agree with some of the points of view expressed. In order to justify your disagreement, you will want to gather facts from other sources to support your opposing points of view.

When you are writing an essay, you are expressing your own opinions. They will carry much more weight, however, if they are backed up by facts. Here's a good example of a strong point of view expressed in essay form in this excerpt from an editorial published in the August 8, 1988, issue of *The New Republic* under the title "Ban Boxing":

In June a number of well-to-do white men came to Atlantic City, intending to watch at close range as two black men spent the better part of an hour trying to knock each other unconscious. But one of the black men was incapacitated after only 91 seconds, and the spectacle ended abruptly. There sat Jack Nicholson, Sean Penn, George Steinbrenner, and Donald Trump—all dressed up and no blood to flow.

Some day, if all goes well, anthropologists will look back at our Society and marvel at the persistent popularity of boxing at this late date in human evolution. The uniqueness of the sport's barbarism lies not in the fact that fighters sometimes die on the job. That's true of football, after all. But boxing is the only modern sport in which the object of the game is to move the opponent closer to death. On this point, Mike Tyson, the man left standing in Atlantic City . . . notes: "This is a hurt business. When you see guys like Trump, Kennedy, and Rockefeller—bluebloods—when they come to a fight, regardless of what they may represent, they come to see someone get hurt, and my objective is to inflict as much punishment as possible."

Tyson, at age 22, is still able to speak in complete sentences, and at normal velocity. But boxers with more ring time behind them aren't always so sharp. Did you see the pictures of Muhammad Ali at the Tyson fight, sitting at ringside and smiling? Sit and smile is one of the few things he can do well these days. He has Parkinson's Syndrome, brought on by years of pounding. This isn't as bad as the severe mental debilitation of "punch drunkenness," which afflicts some former fighters. But Ali's speech is slow and slurred, and these days it takes him a good while to conceive and spit out a ditty on par with, "Float like a butterfly, sting like a bee."

What were the facts used in this excerpt to make a point? In sequential order they include:

1. The boxing match in Atlantic City attracted wealthy and prominent men. (Movie stars Jack Nicholson and Sean Penn, the owner of the New York Yankees baseball team, George Steinbrenner, and millionaire casino owner Donald Trump are mentioned.)

2. The fight ended after ninety-one seconds because one of the boxers was too physically disabled to continue.

3. Boxing "is the only modern sport in which the object of the game is to move the opponent closer to death." (Presented as fact, but arguable.)

4. Former boxing champion Muhammad Ali suffers from Parkinson's Syndrome as a result of boxing.

5. Some former fighters suffer from severe mental debilitation.

Obviously the writer of this editorial took a strong point of view and reinforced it with a selection of facts to convince the reader that his point of view was correct: that boxing is a brutal sport and should be banned.

THE GATHERING OF FACTS

You will need to make good use of facts to make your point whether you are writing a research or term paper, composing a speech, or making notes for a debate. One famous example of the gathering of facts to make a point is Florence Nightingale's *Notes on Matters Affecting the Health, Efficiency, and Hospital Administration of the British Army*, published in 1857. This report was based on her experiences as a nurse at Scutari and Balaclava—on Russia's Crimean Peninsula, extending into the Black Sea—during the Crimean War (1853-56). The 230,000-word document was so thoroughly researched, and her points so strongly made, that it resulted in a revolution in sanitation, hygiene, medical care, and hospital administration, bringing new stature to the nursing profession.

She could never forget the horror of the conditions she found among the sick and wounded when she arrived in the Crimea. The mortality rate was high, but through her efforts at improved hygiene, sanitation, and diet, the mortality rate declined markedly.

In her notes she described the life of the soldier, including his food and clothing as well as his psychological and moral health. She wrote about one typical soldier:

He wore, during the winter, a single pair of laced boots, which, being wet through, he was afraid to unlace, lest the heat of the tent should dry them, so that they could not be put on again. Thus, even when asked by the Regimental Surgeon, he denied that he felt numbness in his feet, lest he should be ordered to unlace his boots.

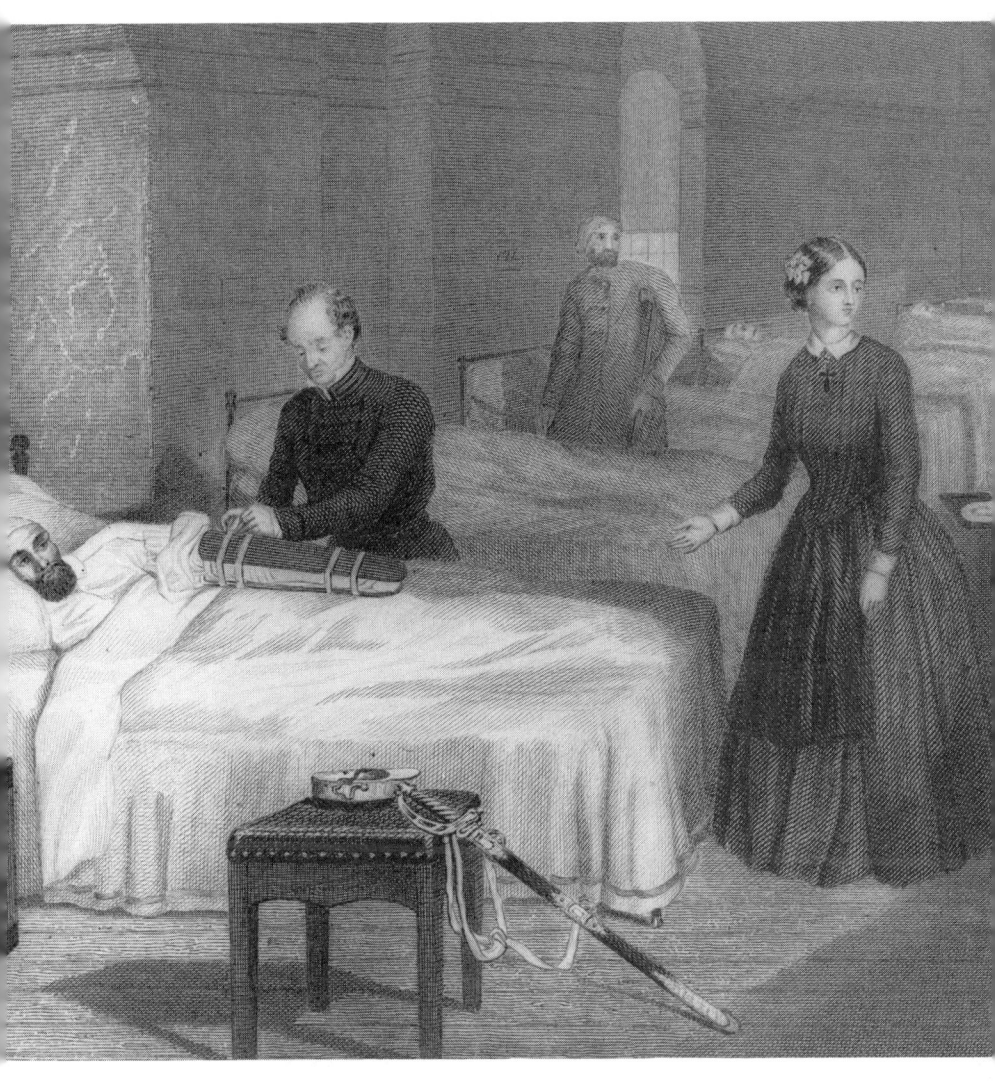

Florence Nightingale, born to wealthy parents, devoted her life to improving the quality of medical care. Her skillful use of the written word led to many reforms.

Florence Nightingale's writings exposed deficiencies in hygiene, sanitation, and diet at hospitals treating Crimean War wounded. This 1850s engraving shows conditions at a hospital in Sebastopol.

She also pointed to the lack of sanitation as the cause of many often-fatal diseases, such as cholera and typhoid fever:

Typhoid fever is well known to be pre-eminently due to foul air, arising from overcrowding and want of drainage; and, till the sanitary works at Scutari were executed, it appears, by Dr. Cumming's own showing, to have prevailed there.

Her all-encompassing *Notes* included every aspect of Army life, always with a view to showing how they affected "the health, efficiency, and hospital administration of the British Army." She prefaced her *Notes* by giving a brief history of the British Army in previous wars; then she described and analyzed the medical history of the Crimean War, including the following subjects:

- Organization of regimental and general hospitals
- The need for sanitary officials and a statistical department
- A survey of the education, employment, and promotion of medical officers
- Soldier's pay
- The diet and cooking of the Army, including recipes (e.g., "cheap plain rice pudding for campaigning")
- Notes on how to set up an encampment
- Washing and canteens
- Soldiers' wives
- Construction of Army hospitals in peace and war, with a summary of "defects and suggestions"

The horror that she experienced in the Crimea she saw as the direct result of the incompetence and criminal negligence of the Army Medical Corps and the War Office. This was "dirt" that she was determined would not be "swept under the rug." The facts that she gathered in great detail and profusion for her *Notes* clearly and convincingly made her point.

INTERPRETATION OF FACTS

In preparing for a debate, you work hard to find the most important facts to strengthen your position. But you also have a number of supporting facts at hand to use when needed in counterattacks against your opponent's arguments. Whatever facts are presented, however, they are always open to "interpretation" to support a particular point of view. For this reason you must make certain that the facts you use are true and that they come from reliable sources; otherwise your argument will be weakened, and you may lose the debate. The same holds true for research papers and speeches. Select the most convincing facts, facts that cannot be distorted, so you will be successful in making your point.

QUOTING OUT OF CONTEXT

The same approach to facts holds for any quoted material you decide to use. Be selective in choosing the strongest quotes you can gather to support your point of view. Also, when using quoted material, you should be careful not to quote out of context. If you are using a quote, use enough of it so that you will avoid misleading or inaccurate statements.

In 1960 some newspapers played up a statement found in an Air Force Reserve training manual. It created a public uproar because it was quoted out of context. The statement quoted was the following:

Another rather foolish remark often heard is that Americans have a right to know what is going on.

This got a stinging reaction because it appeared to be a military policy in direct opposition to the public's right to know what its government, including the military, is doing.

What was omitted from the quote was the following explanation:

Most people realize the foolhardiness of such a suggestion. If a football team should start telling the other side the plays it planned to use, their opponents would sweep them off the field. It's the same in war—hot or cold; if we tell our secrets, we are likely to be beaten, and beaten badly.

This makes the (complete) Air Force statement reasonable and acceptable, particularly in light of the fact that at that time the United States was engaged in a bitter Cold War (a state of political tension and military rivalry between nations, stopping short of actual full-scale war) with the Soviet Union, with deep suspicion and mutual distrust on both sides.

Remember, therefore, that often "text out of context is pretext." In other words if only part of a quote is used, it can often be misleading or dishonest because the full meaning and intent of the statement has not been revealed.

THE SKILLFUL USE OF LOGIC

3

Whenever you are defending your point of view, whether in a research paper, speech, or informal or formal debate, you must use logical arguments as well as facts to support it. The word *logic* has its root in the Greek word *logikē*, which means "the art of reasoning." A more contemporary definition of logic is "valid reasoning, especially as distinguished from invalid or irrational argumentation." The word *argumentation* used in this definition is the key to any understanding of the use of logic because logic is basically concerned with arguments used to defend a point of view. The more logical the arguments, the better able you will be to convince others of the reasonableness of your point of view, whether they agree with it or not.

DEDUCTIVE AND INDUCTIVE REASONING

Two common methods of logical argument are deductive and inductive reasoning. In deductive reasoning you begin with a generalization and then mention specific facts to prove your point. A simple bare bones example of deductive reasoning is the following:

> All men are mortal.
> Socrates is a man.
> Therefore Socrates is mortal.

When you are using deductive reasoning, however, you may be using the same basic approach as that in the above example, but your reasoning process will involve a much more complex outpouring of words. A case in point is the trial of suffragist Susan B. Anthony, who in 1872—along with fifteen other women from Rochester, New York—had voted illegally in the presidential election (women at that time were denied the right to vote). Not only was she not permitted to testify in her defense; the jury was not allowed to deliberate the case because the judge instructed them to find a verdict of guilty. Anthony finally got a chance to speak when the judge asked her: "Has the prisoner anything to say why sentence should not be pronounced?" What followed was a passionate defense of the constitutional right of all citizens—including women—to vote, and this defense represented deductive reasoning. The generalization she used as the focus of her argument was that the U.S. Constitution guarantees every citizen the right to vote. Women are citizens; therefore, women have the right to vote. She also mentioned other citizen's rights that had been denied her. Here are some excerpts:

Your denial of my citizen's right to vote is the denial of my right of consent as one of the governed, the denial of my right to trial by a jury of my peers as an

Women's rights activist Susan B. Anthony (1820–1906) argued passionately in defense of the Constitutional rights of all citizens.

offender against the law, the denial of my sacred rights to life, liberty, property and [at this point she was interrupted by the judge who tried to stop her from speaking]...

All my prosecutors, from the 8th ward corner grocery store politician, who entered the complaint, to the United States Marshal, Commissioner, District Attorney, District Judge, Your Honor on the bench, not one is my peer, but each and all my political sovereigns [because they had the right to vote, a right denied to her as a woman]; and had Your Honor submitted my case to the jury, as was clearly your duty, even then I should have had just cause of protest, for not one of those men was my peer; but, native or foreign, white or black, rich or poor, educated or ignorant, awake or asleep, sober or drunk, each and every man of them was my political superior; hence, in no sense, my peer.

When the judge explained that she had been tried according to established forms of law, she replied:

Yes, Your Honor, but by forms of law all made by men, interpreted by men, administered by men, in favor of men, and against women; and hence your Honor's ordered verdict of guilty, against a United States citizen for the exercise of that "citizen's right to vote," simply because that citizen was a woman and not a man.

EXAMPLE OF INDUCTIVE REASONING

An example of inductive reasoning, in which you begin with specific examples and end with a conclusion or generalization, is the following excerpt from a discussion of the importance of using precise language when making a will*:

A man who was a millionaire when he made his will left $100,000 to a university and the "residue of the estate" to his children. Unintentionally he cut them off with nothing when it was discovered after his death that the value of his assets had fallen below $100,000. Another man left a yearly income to his married niece "as long as she is above ground." When she died her husband installed her in a mausoleum above ground and collected the money for the rest of his life.

This discussion ended with the following conclusion: "In preparing a will, it is vital that you spell out the desires specifically and unmistakably, leaving nothing to chance."

ILLOGICAL THINKING

In using logic to make your point, you should take care to avoid a number of traps, including the following.

Self-Contradiction
Example: Computer technology is the most important development in the world of business because it has saved tremendous time in many business operations, lowered costs, and made it possible for many businesses to operate with fewer employees. In spite of these advantages, however, I think the new developments in telecommunications are more important.
Comment: The writer is contradicting herself and

---

*Henry V. Poor, Advisory Editor, *You and the Law* (Pleasantville, New York: Reader's Digest Association, 1977).

confusing the reader, who will wonder which really is the most important development, computer technology or telecommunications.

Reasoning in a Circle
Example: The trade unions believe that workers should have more control of the business that employs them because no business could operate without them. Businesses should do what the trade unions want them to do because they couldn't operate without workers. *Comment:* Instead of elaborating on the point made in the first sentence, the writer repeats what was said originally.

Hasty Generalization
Example: Helen Keller was blind and deaf since infancy, but she became a famous author and lecturer in spite of these handicaps. This proves that anyone who suffers from a handicap can overcome it and have an outstanding career. *Comment:* The writer is leaping to an illogical conclusion. Not all handicapped people can overcome their handicaps or have careers or professions.

Illogical Assumption
or Implication
Example: The book tells the story of a very tense and poignant drama, although when I finished reading it, I was left with a feeling of completeness and satisfaction. *Comment:* The writer illogically assumes that a tense, poignant drama does not leave the reader with a feeling of completeness or satisfaction.

Unwarranted Deduction
Example: Because Robert Louis Stevenson was not as physically healthy and active as his friends, he thought and wrote more than they did. *Comment:*

"Let's get one thing clear: Is this discussion going to be conducted in vague generalities or specific generalities?"

The illogic here is in inferring that the first fact was the cause of the second. People in poor health do not necessarily think and write more than those who are in good health.

Gap in Thought
Example: She disapproves of Democrats, especially the huge budget deficit. *Comment:* The gap in thought here is between "Democrats" and "budget deficit." The writer is mixing apples and oranges. She may have intended to say that the person described disapproved of members of the Democratic Party because she blamed them for the nation's budget deficit, but how is the reader to know this until the gap is filled?

Reasoning Beside the Point
Example: The hero of *Catcher in the Rye* is a misfit who rebels against authority and refuses to act responsibly. He fails courses in school and drops out not because he isn't smart enough but because he refuses to do the work expected of him. If schools had better teachers, there wouldn't be so many dropouts. *Comment:* The last sentence has nothing to do with the stated reasons for the hero's dropping out of school.

Quoting Biased Authority
As Henry Stillwell, one of the most outspoken leaders in the black power movement, points out in his article, white leaders have never extended a helping hand to blacks. *Comment:* This is an exaggerated example, but it underscores the need not to take any writer's (or authority's) words as completely true and fair unless they are supported by facts.

Here are examples of several errors in logic from a "Firing Line" debate held May 27, 1987, in New York

City, on the question, "Are We Getting Anywhere in the U.N.?" The participants were United Nations Ambassador Vernon Walters and Ernest Van Den Haag, co-author with John P. Conrad of the book, *The United Nations: In or Out?* At one point in the debate Professor Van Den Haag asked Ambassador Walters: "Do you foresee that the Soviet Union, China, the United States, Cuba, whatnot, will give up any of their sovereignty in favor of some sort of super-government (i.e., a United Nations with the power to make and enforce international decisions affecting individual countries) and would you favor that?" Ambassador Walters responded:

"No, I would not. But I don't believe any of the regimes that you have mentioned . . . will do that. [gap in thought] But [the totalitarian states] they're doomed. They're doomed. If you look at the whole course of human history, that course has been upward toward greater dignity and freedom for the individual man. Many tyrannies in the past have temporarily halted that flow. None of them have permanently halted it. And these modern tyrannies—these medieval tyrannies masquerading in modern garb as progressive regimes—are not going to escape from the inevitable laws of history. The principal things we want to do are two things: preserve peace without losing freedom and justice." [gap in thought]

"And I would cite you, for instance, one of the reasons why we preserve peace [in Europe] is that we maintain the tremendous sacrifice of the armed forces which we [as a member of NATO, the North Atlantic Treaty Organization] support, which is the most important thing. The other thing is if you limit it to that, you're limiting it to Western Europe, and none of the countries would be willing to extend it elsewhere. So you've got to take what you find in place, which is the United Nations, and try to shape it into something like that." ⎯ hasty generalization and self-contradiction

LOGICAL THINKING

You don't have to study the laws of logic in order to write logically in making your point, but it is important for you to be able to test the logic or reasonableness of what you are trying to say. When you present arguments to support your point of view, they must be logical. In other words they must appear reasonable to you before you present them to the reader or the audience. This means you must think logically and be convinced of the logic of your arguments when writing and revising your research paper, speech, or notes for a debate.

Incompleteness of thought often gets in the way of logical thinking. When you present an argument, think it through. Check yourself to see if you have included and responded to all aspects of that particular argument. For example, suppose you are writing a research paper on military service and you take the point of view that no young person should be forced into military service against his or her will. You could argue that spending a year or two in the army, navy, or air force is an unwarranted interruption in a young person's plans for college or a career. You argue that the needs of the military can be met with volunteers, if enough incentives are offered.

But your thought—and your logic—are on hazardous ground if you ignore situations in which global

politics, an international crisis, or the threat of war make it necessary to maintain large and strong military forces to meet this danger, even when the outbreak of war seems unlikely.

To think and write logically you should also take pains to use enough words, and the right words, to express your meaning. Make sure that your thought is complete and expressed as clearly as possible. What you say may be grammatically correct, properly spelled and punctuated, but it will fall far short of your intent if the thought or argument is not complete or clearly stated.

THE SKILLFUL USE OF LANGUAGE

4

In their book *Writing and Thinking*, Norman Foerster and J. M. Steadman, Jr., addressed the problem of writing in this way:

> *Given*: a thought or feeling
> *Required*: words that will express this thought or feeling and convey it to the reader unchanged
> *The solution*: The words required for the expression of thought or feeling are the words inherent in the thought or feeling itself. They are not cunningly devised by the writer, invented and arranged by him with a view to impressing the reader. He does nothing but find them in the place where they spring to life, that is, in the mind.

At first reading this formula may appear to be an oversimplification of how to overcome the problem of writing well, until you think about the ideas expressed. The language you select or use, no matter what you're writing, must relate to the subject, and it must come from your experience with words. These are words that you use in everyday speech, words you have read in a multiplicity of sources—newspapers, magazines, books—and words you have heard spoken by others—for example, by public speakers such as politicians, by authorities in fields such as education, science, and the fine arts, and by actors and actresses in movies, television and the theater. From all of these experiences you select those words that are most appropriate to the task at hand.

Suppose your assignment is to write an essay on friendship—for example, "How to Make Friends and Keep Them." What words would come to mind? If you have a close friend, your thoughts may go back to when you first met and decided to become friends. These thoughts might suggest the following words and phrases: someone my own age—pleasant to look at and be with—good sense of humor—things that struck both of us as funny—interests in common—things we like to do together—sports, music, movies.

When you think about why the friendship has lasted, some of these words and phrases might come to mind: being able to share confidences—when we disagree about someone or something, never staying mad—loyalty—taking my side when someone is down on me—sympathizing with me when I am troubled or something unfortunate happens to me—always ready to help when it's needed—planning things to do together—never being jealous or petty, always wishing the best for each other.

The same thought processes will be involved

whatever subject you happen to be writing or speaking about. If it's a research paper for a course in psychology, the words you select will come from the material you have read as well as from your personal experiences, if you choose (or are expected) to use one or more personal examples in making your point.

If you're writing a speech or making notes for a debate about a controversial topic—such as (either for or against) the legalization of marijuana—the same holds true. You will find the appropriate words in the material you read and from your personal experience.

THE POWER OF LANGUAGE

Throughout the history of the world, the power of language has proved the aptness of the statement, "The pen is mightier than the sword."* It required a tremendous military effort on the part of the Allies to achieve victory in World War II, but it was an inspiration and a driving incentive for American troops, their loved ones, and all Americans to know that they were fighting for "The Four Freedoms" designated in 1941 by President Franklin D. Roosevelt: "Freedom of Speech, Freedom of Religion, Freedom from Want, Freedom from Fear." Billboards throughout the nation proclaimed this message until the war ended in 1945.

The power of language is a part of everyday living and influences us in many ways. What you learn in school, what your parents have taught you, what you learn about religion, the clothes you wear, the food you eat, the entertainment you enjoy—all depend to

---

*Edward Bulwer Lytton, from his play *Richelieu*, Act II, Scene 2 (1839).

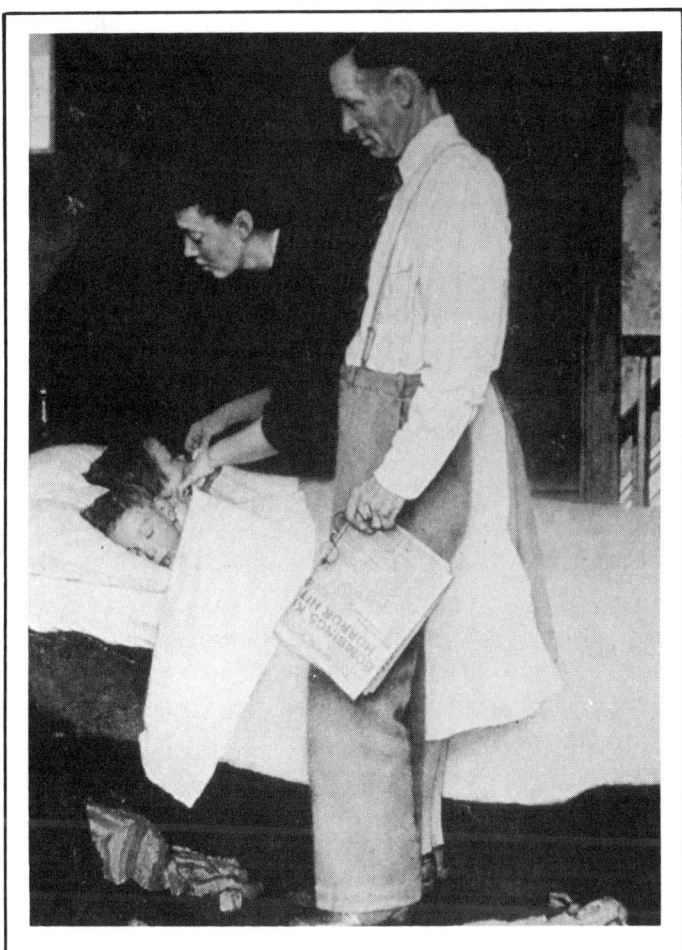

FREEDOM FROM FEAR

President Roosevelt's "Four Freedoms," freedom of speech, freedom of religion, freedom from want, and freedom from fear, inspired Americans during the Second World War. Artist Norman Rockwell gave them visual form.

some extent on the power of language. Political slogans help to decide elections. Movie ads help you to decide which movies you want to see. Manufacturers of all the products you buy spend millions of dollars trying to find the most persuasive words to use in advertising their products.

HONING YOUR LANGUAGE SKILLS: CONCISENESS

One essential quality of good writing is conciseness; the author must be able to omit unnecessary words. When you are writing, the most important thing is to get all the ideas down on paper in a "rough draft." For someone who wants to learn how to write well, developing proper sentence and paragraph form and logical sequence is the first and most difficult step, but only the first step. The next step is to revise what has been written, deleting the unnecessary ideas and words. Check the sense to make sure you are saying what you mean to say to the best of your ability. Then add ideas and thoughts where needed to strengthen your point of view.

Writing concisely means avoiding wordiness. In the book he co-authored with William Strunk, Jr., *Elements of Style*,* E.B. White showed the difference between wordiness and conciseness:

(wordiness)

Macbeth was very ambitious. This led him to wish to become king of Scotland. The witches told him that this wish of his would come true. The King of Scotland at this time was Duncan. Encouraged by his

---

*William Strunk, Jr., and E.B. White, *Elements of Style* (New York: Macmillan Publishing Co., 1979).

E.B. White, shown here in 1954 at his office at the New Yorker *magazine, was a master prose stylist. His* Elements of Style, *coauthored with William Strunk, Jr., is required reading for writers.*

"A lot has happened since our last meeting."

wife, Macbeth murdered Duncan. He was thus able to succeed Duncan as king.
(51 words)

(conciseness)

Encouraged by his wife, Macbeth achieved his ambition and realized the prediction of the witches by murdering Duncan and becoming king of Scotland in his place.
(26 words)

It is not easy to learn how to write concisely, but it is the goal of every writer who wants to write well. This means that you must learn not only how to omit unnecessary words but also how to construct interesting sentences. Sometimes, as in the first example above, you may take several sentences to say what could be said concisely—and interestingly—in one. In the first example six sentences were used. In the second example only one sentence was used. The first example is not only wordy, it is boring to read. The second example is concise and interestingly expressed.

PUTTING VIGOR INTO YOUR WRITING

You can make your writing vigorous and interesting by writing all positive statements in a positive way, by avoiding negatives, and also by using the active voice (in which the subject acts) rather than the passive voice (in which the subject is acted upon). Here's an example of an unnecessarily negative sentence:

At archery practice Roy was not able to hit the bull's-eye very often.

Here it is again, this time cast positively:

At archery practice Roy usually missed the bull's-eye.

This second version is direct, vigorous, and expressive. The first version, by comparison, is a weak and sluggish way of saying the same thing. It also uses more words: fourteen. The concise, positive statement uses nine words. What also makes the first version weak is that it tells the reader what the person did not do, while the second version tells the reader what the person did, which makes the statement direct and emphatic.

It is an important rule to keep in mind that the active voice is usually more direct and vigorous than the passive voice. Here's a sentence in which the passive voice is used:

The first time I let Harry borrow money will always be regretted by me.

Note how much more vigorous and interesting the sentence is when put in the active voice:

I will always regret the first time I let Harry borrow money.

It is not only more vigorous, it even has an element of suspense. The reader immediately wants to know what happened because it is leading directly into the next thought.

WORD CHOICE:
USING PRECISE LANGUAGE

A lazy writer lets the words fall where they may in a rambling, disorganized outpouring of random thoughts. A careful writer is one who takes the trouble to write clearly by organizing thoughts in a logical progression and by choosing words with care. There will be moments when you can't think of the exact word you want to use, or you try using a word and then worry about its appropriateness. Using the wrong words can distort the meaning of what you want to convey to the reader or audience.

Your first recourse should be to use the dictionary. This will not only give you the exact meaning of the word you had in mind but will suggest others that might be more appropriate to your thought and meaning. If you can't find what you want quickly enough in the dictionary, other good sources are *Roget's Thesaurus* or some other dictionary of synonyms. One of the great delights of the English language is the tremendous variety in choice of words and meanings.

For example, the word *droop* seems simple enough, but look at the range of meanings (and examples) in the *American Heritage Dictionary*:

> *droop* (droop) v. (verb) *drooped*, *drooping*, *droops*. intran. [intransitive—does not take an object] 1. To bend or hang downward; sag: "his mouth dropped sadly, pulled down, no doubt, by the plump weight of his jowls" (Gore Vidal). 2. To sag in dejection, exhaustion, or lifelessness: "The roses drooped in the heat, their petals scattering" (Herman Wouk)—Tran. [transitive—takes an object] To let bend or hang down: "He drooped his body over the rail" (Norman Mailer).—noun. The act or condition of drooping.

You should also be aware of the connotation or suggested meaning of words because many words suggest more than they literally mean. This is another good reason for you to check the dictionary when you are not sure of the exact meaning of a word or how it should most appropriately be used. It can also help you to avoid *malapropism*, using a word that sounds like the word you have in mind but means something totally different.

Malapropisms are often used by comedians and others for humor. For example, the following statements were attributed to a baseball coach whose hobby was malapropisms (the words that should have been used are in brackets): "This is the crutch [crux] of the problem."—"He has a chronicle [chronic] knee injury."—"We're changing our floor mat [format] this week."

When they are used intentionally, malapropisms may be funny, but if you make this kind of mistake, you will simply look foolish. For example, the words *allusion*, *elusion*, and *illusion* are often confused. *Allusion* means "an indirect reference, a hint;" *elusion* means "a clever escape, evasion;" *illusion* means "a misleading image or vision." All of these words sound similar, but note the sharp differences in meaning.

APPROPRIATE USE OF POETIC LANGUAGE

There may be times when you will want to color or dramatize your writing to make it more interesting or to emphasize a point you are trying to make. You may then want to make use of a figure of speech. This is an expression in which words are used not in their literal sense but to create a more forceful or dramatic image. The most commonly used figures of speech are metaphors, similes, and hyperboles.

A metaphor is a figure of speech in which a term

ordinarily used of one thing is applied to another by implied comparison or analogy. For instance, we speak of "the curtain of night" and "the enfolding arms of sleep."

In a simile two essentially unlike things are compared, as in the following quote from Gore Vidal: "Like ancient trees, we die from the top." The inference here is that, as people become elderly, they begin to lose their mental faculties, as in senility. A hyperbole is an exaggeration or extravagant statement used as a figure of speech, such as "I could sleep forever" and "This book weighs a ton."

AVOIDING SLANG, JARGON, AND CLICHÉS

Slang words may be appropriate in some instances, as long as you are certain that your reader or audience will understand what they mean (or if you define exactly what you mean), but in general, using slang shows both laziness of thought and poverty of vocabulary.

Jargon is nonsensical, incoherent, or meaningless speech. The specialized or technical language of a trade, profession, or science is also referred to as jargon. When you use this kind of language, you will need to explain what it means to the reader or audience unfamiliar with it.

A cliché is a trite or overworked expression or idea. It has been used so much that it either has lost its meaning and relevance or has become a dull, boring expression. Here are a few examples: *method to his madness*; *last but not least*; *good as gold*; *crazy as a loon*; *point in time*; *acid test*; *clear as a bell*. In revising what you have written, when you discover that you have used a cliché, find a fresh way of saying what you really mean.

Use of clichés and jargon can give a speech a "canned" quality.

DEVELOPING A WRITING STYLE

Commenting on writing style, E.B. White said, "Every writer, by the way he uses language, reveals something of his spirit, his habits, his capacities, his bias. This is inevitable as well as enjoyable." If you want to develop a good writing style, you must make use of all the elements of writing technique, observing the prohibitions already mentioned. However, you must also write in a way that comes naturally, being careful not to overwrite or to overstate the subject of your composition. Something else to keep in mind is to avoid using a breezy manner or assuming some other attitude that will get in the way of what you are trying to say in making your point.

One of the most admired twentieth-century writers was the Englishman George Orwell, two of whose books are considered classics (*1984* and *Animal Farm*). What he had to say in his essay "Politics and the English Language" is as relevant now as it was then:

Modern writing at its worst does not consist in picking out words for the sake of their meaning and inventing images in order to make the meaning clearer. It consists in gumming together long strips of words which have already been set in order by someone else, and making the results presentable by pure humbug. The attraction of this way of writing is that it is easy. It is easier—even quicker, once you have the habit—to say In my opinion it is not an unjustifiable assumption that *than to say* I think.

He advised writers who want to write with clarity and emphasis to ask themselves four questions each time they attempt to write a sentence:

1. What am I trying to say?
2. What words will express it?

3. What image or idiom will make it clearer?
4. Is this image fresh enough to have an effect?

MAKING YOUR MESSAGE CLEAR

What all successful speakers and writers have in common is their ability to make their message clear. Whether you're writing an essay, research paper, speech, or commentary for a debate, you need to make your message clear so your point of view, your logic and arguments, will be understood. The devices you use will depend on the subject matter of your discussion as well as your audience (teacher, fellow students, general public etc.).

If there is a need to use technical terms that are unfamiliar to your audience, you have an obligation to explain them. However, this should be done in as few words as possible so as not to interfere with the thrust and flow of your arguments. As pointed out earlier, careful attention to the meaning of words is also important. You should use words that accurately reflect the meaning you wish to convey. When in doubt, check the definitions in your dictionary.

EXPLAINING WHAT YOU MEAN

The confusion inherent in words and phrases can be seen in the Christian dictum: "Love your enemies." Clergyman Ralph Sockman once offered the following explanation. "In the New Testament there are two Greek words translated into our one word 'love.' Therein lies the confusion." He then went on to explain that the Greek words were *phileo*, which means intimate emotional affection, and *agapo*, which means an attitude of active goodwill. When Christ asked his followers to love their enemies, he meant love in the sense of the Greek word *agapo.* Sockman concluded: "To love your enemy does not mean that you agree with what he thinks or like what he does, or even that you like his personal qualities, but that you have an attitude of goodwill toward him and seek his highest good."

COMPARISON AND CONTRAST

Another way to promote clarity is to use comparison and contrast to emphasize differences. Ford Elvridge, when he was governor of Guam, made good use of this device in a discussion on the differences between education and wisdom. Among other examples he offered the following:

Education teaches us that two and two make four. But wisdom teaches us that you cannot get more than two and two out of four. Education informs us that the first atom bombs were dropped on Hiroshima and Nagasaki in the year 1945. But wisdom teaches us that man has created a force with which he may destroy civilization.

DEFINITION BY EXAMPLE

Another way to make your meaning clear is to use a good example. The American Medical Association defines a psychosomatic disorder as a physical illness caused by a mental or emotional problem. It goes on to point out that the illness is real, not imaginary, but can often be cured by treatment of the underlying psychological problem.

Here are excerpts from an example that a physician, Dr. John Schindler, used to illustrate what is meant by psychosomatic illness in an address to a lay (nonmedical) audience at Ohio State University.

The subject of his illustration was a grocer who complained of stomach pain but was told repeatedly by medical experts that it was not caused by a physical problem, such as an ulcer.

He was in competition with the chain stores, and he had a wife who—well, I believe if I'd have had his wife, I'd have had his pain. And as if that wasn't enough for anybody, he had a son who was always getting into trouble. Not just a little trouble, but a whole lot of trouble! And between the three—his business, his wife, and his son—he had this pain in the stomach most of the time.

After being told there was apparently no physical problem causing the pain, Dr. Schindler continued:

He finally began to believe himself that he didn't have it, because every time he went up north fishing, which was twice a year, all he had to do was get to Belleville, which is 25 miles north of Monroe (his home), and his pain stopped. And it didn't come back again until he got to Round Grove Hill on the way home where he could see the court house tower, and right there his pain started.

THE VIRTUES OF SIMPLICITY AND DIRECTNESS

Whatever devices you choose to use or that seem most appropriate as well as important in making your point, always keep in mind the virtues of simplicity and directness. This does not mean that you should write as you speak, because when we speak to one another we do not usually speak in clear, well-organized thoughts, nor do we necessarily use the best words to make our meaning clear to the listener.

However, as in conversation, you should select words that you feel comfortable with, as long as they express your thoughts clearly and completely.

Simplicity of language, moreover, does not mean that you should use as many one- or two-syllable words as possible. If the words you use are appropriate to the subject, you have achieved simplicity of expression. But if you use certain words because you think they will impress the reader or listener, you may succeed only in clouding your thoughts and confusing the reader. Your goal should be to make it possible for the reader or listener to understand what you are saying as effortlessly as possible.

It is for this same reason that you should aim at directness of expression. This means organizing your thoughts in a logical progression and keeping to the subject. Don't introduce thoughts, issues, or arguments that have little bearing on the subject you are discussing. Length in itself will not impress the reader. On the other hand, in aiming for directness of expression you should keep conscious of the need to make your thoughts as complete as possible. When you have finished your first draft, read it carefully for sense and note where a thought or argument needs some additional work to make a point.

RHYTHM, SOUND, SYNTAX

Other things to look for when you are revising your first draft are the rhythm of your sentences, the sound of the words, and your syntax—the way in which you have put words together to form phrases and sentences. Your variety of sentence structure will determine the kind of rhythm you have achieved. If you've used several short, simple sentences in sequence (as in E. B. White's first example on *Macbeth*), the rhythm will be choppy. But if you use a good mix of simple, compound, and complex sentences, the rhythm will be smooth and satisfying.

Rhythm in itself, in fact, can add interest to what you have to say because it makes the reading easy and enjoyable. When you are reading the draft of a paper you have written, make a conscious effort to listen to the rhythm of the syntax (you might even want to read the paper out loud). Then make improvements when the rhythm seems too abrupt or too long. Maintaining good variety of sentence structure provides not only a pleasing flow of words but the pauses a reader needs to "breathe" between thoughts. Here's an example from my book on debating*:

One recommended technique is to utter the words in a major argument with concentrated deliberation. Stop abruptly and pause in the right places. Use a natural gesture to attract attention. Lower your tone and slow the rate of delivery, or increase the volume and pace. Anything you can do to increase the attention of judge and audience to your main points will help you give them the emphasis they deserve.

The first sentence is a fairly long simple sentence of fifteen words. The next two sentences are short, simple sentences of eight and seven words, respectively. The next sentence is a compound sentence of sixteen words. The last sentence is a complex sentence that begins with a noun clause and includes twenty-five words. This is a short paragraph with five sentences and seventy-one words. The variety in sentence structure and in words per sentence (fifteen,

---

*Robert E. Dunbar, *How to Debate* (New York: Franklin Watts, 1987).

eight, seven, sixteen, twenty-five) encourages ease of reading, adds interest to the thoughts expressed, and emphasizes the point being made.

THE SOUND OF WORDS

The sound of words you use is also important. You need to vary sound as well as sentence structure to make your writing interesting and enjoyable to read. If you have too many words that sound alike—unless you are trying to achieve a particular effect—your writing will sound monotonous. Note the sounds in the following sentence:

The revolution that led to civil war produced a constitution that failed to bring any resolution to the people's problems.

There are too many *shun* sounds (words that end in *-tion*) in this sentence: *revolution*, *constitution*, and *resolution*. There are also too many *th* words, which give a thick sound to the sentence. Here is the same thought expressed in a better variety of sounds:

A new constitution was approved when the civil war ended, but it failed to solve the people's problems.

SOUND-ALIKE WORDS

As a general rule, when you can do so without changing or distorting the meaning of a sentence, it is a good idea to avoid using too many words with similar sounds or sound-alike words that might confuse the reader. Here are several pairs of sound-alike words that might inadvertently be used too close together in the same sentence and cause confusion: *accept* and *except*; *adapt* and *adopt*; *affect* and *effect*; *conscience* and *conscious*; *fare* and *fair*; *hear* and *here*; *peace* and *piece*; *weather* and *whether*. There are many more.

A careful writer will be alert to the need to make appropriate changes when she discovers she has used words that have similar sounds or sound-alike words that interfere with the clear expression of her thoughts.

APPEALING TO THE EMOTIONS

5

In your attempts to persuade reader or audience to accept your point of view, you may want to make a conscious appeal to the emotions. The particular emotions involved will depend on the subject, your point of view, and your audience. Some topics are themselves emotional. Just the mention of them evokes an immediate emotional response. Among these are politics, religion, poverty, crime, and sex, to name a few. Before anyone reads or hears what you have to say, an immediate emotional response is aroused once the subject is known.

In presenting your point of view, you will be using your language skills to evoke the intended emotional responses that will bring reader or listener to accept your ideas. The range of possible responses is broad: love, hate, fear, anxiety, envy, jealousy, sympathy, hostility, frustration, hope, resignation, and many more. Depending on your subject and point of view, what you are writing about may be intended to arouse several emotions, ending, of course, with approval for your point of view. You may want to base your piece on either your personal experience or someone else's, using the narrative technique.

THE NARRATIVE TECHNIQUE

Long before the Civil War, many abolitionist groups recruited speakers to promote the antislavery cause. The following excerpt from a speech by an escaped Negro slave, Lewis Clark, was delivered in 1843 to an audience in Maine.

How would you like to have your wives, your daughters, your sisters completely, totally in the power of a master? I had a pretty sister; she was whiter than I am, for she took after her father. When she was sixteen years old, her master sent for her. When he sent again, she cried, and didn't want to go. She told her mother her troubles, and she tried to encourage her to be decent, and hold up her head if she could. Her master was so mad to think she complained to her mother, that he sold her right off to Louisiana, and we heard afterward that she died there of hard usage.

Here a narrative account was used to illustrate one of the evils of slavery: sexual abuse. The audience was immediately able to identify with some of the words the speaker used, such as "wives, daughters, and sisters." Some of the expressions, such as "totally in the power of a master," also had strong emotional appeal; in relating how his sister had turned to her mother for help, "she tried to encourage her to be decent, and hold up her head if she could"; and in relating the young woman's fate, "died there of hard usage."

THE EMOTIONAL POWER IN "CIVIL DISOBEDIENCE"

Three years after Lewis Clark had given his impassioned and pathetic account of the evils of slavery, a famous incident occurred which resulted in a speech and essay which has affected the world profoundly down to the present day. One night in July 1846, Henry David Thoreau, the philosopher, poet, and author of *Walden*, was arrested for nonpayment of the poll tax* in Concord, Massachusetts. Rather than pay the tax, he went to jail in protest against the U.S. war with Mexico, which he believed was started by the United States on behalf of slaveholders who wanted to extend their slave territory.

He spent only one night in jail; his tax was paid by a mysterious "veiled lady," and he was released. This experience inspired him to write his famous essay "Civil Disobedience," presented initially as a lecture or speech and later published as an essay. Here are excerpts:

Under a government which imprisons any unjustly, the true place for a just man is also a prison. The proper place today, the only place which Massachusetts has provided for her freer and less desponding spirits, is in her prisons, to be put out and locked out of the state by her own act, as they have already put themselves out by their principles. It is there that the fugitive slave, and the Mexican prisoner on parole, and the Indian come to plead the wrongs of his race should find them; on that separate, but more free and honorable ground, where the State places those who

---

*A tax that was levied on persons rather than property. Payment of this tax was often a requirement for voting.

Henry David Thoreau (1817–1862) spent a famous night in jail for refusing to pay a poll tax to support the Mexican War, which he viewed as an attempt to increase the number of slaveholding states.

are not with her, but against her,—the only house in a slave State in which a free man can abide with honor.

A minority is powerless while it conforms to the majority; it is not even a minority then; but it is irresistible when it clogs by its whole weight. If the alternative is to keep all just men in prison, or give up war and slavery, the State will not hesitate which to choose. If a thousand men were not to pay their tax-bills this year, that would not be a violent and bloody measure, as it would be to pay them, and enable the State to commit violence and shed innocent blood. This is, in fact, the definition of a peaceable revolution, if any such is possible. If the tax-gatherers, or any other public officer asks me, as one has done, "But what shall I do?" my answer is, "If you really wish to do anything, resign your office."

When the subject has refused allegiance, and the officer has resigned his office, then the revolution is accomplished. But even suppose blood should flow. Is there not a sort of blood shed when the conscience is wounded? Through this wound a man's real manhood and immortality flow out, and he bleeds to everlasting death. I see this blood flowing now.

Mahatma Gandhi, who led the fight to win India's independence from Great Britain, first became aware of Thoreau's essay on civil disobedience while fighting for the rights of Indians in South Africa in the early part of this century. He not only adopted some of Thoreau's ideas, he based his movement, Satyagraha, in part on the *peaceable revolution* or "civil disobedience" proclaimed in Thoreau's essay. Satyagraha was a three-pronged movement that included passive resistance, noncooperation, and civil disobedience. In his book, *Non-Violent Resistance*,* Gandhi called civil disobedience "a branch of Satyagraha."

Martin Luther King, Jr., the black civil rights leader who rose to prominence in the 1960s through his nonviolent resistance movement, read Thoreau's essay while in college. He became "fascinated by the idea of refusing to cooperate with an evil system." Words really can change the course of history.

THE EMOTIONAL "I"

When you put yourself in the forefront of the subject you are discussing, you are using the emotional *I* technique. There are several reasons why you might want to use this device. One is to use a personal experience to reinforce your point of view. This tells the reader or audience that you are arguing from your own experience as well as that of others. You know what you are talking about because what you say is based on personal experience.

This technique can also be used effectively to win the sympathy of reader or audience. A good example of this is the speech of General Douglas MacArthur at a joint session of Congress on April 19, 1951. He had just been relieved of his command of U.S. and Allied troops in Korea during the Korean War (1950–53) by President Harry S. Truman. MacArthur had spoken at length in defense of his military strategies and was making a final plea for sympathy and support. This was, in effect, his farewell address to the nation as a military commander, although there was

---

*M.K. Gandhi, *Non-Violent Resistance (Satyagraha)* (New York: Schocken Books, 1961).

still the possibility of a political career should he win enough national support.

His speech elicited a tremendous emotional response, even tears, among some of those who heard it. One of the reasons for the intensity of the emotional response was that MacArthur placed himself squarely in the center of the issues he was discussing by frequent personal references to himself, his career, and his military policies. Here are a few examples:

I address you with neither rancor nor bitterness in the fading twilight of life, but with one purpose in mind: To serve my country.

Efforts have been made to distort my position. It has been said in effect that I was a warmonger. Nothing could be further from the truth. I know war as few other men now living know it, and nothing to me is more revolting. I have long advocated its complete abolition, as its very destructiveness on both friend and foe has rendered it useless as a means of settling international disputes.

I have just left your fighting sons in Korea. They have done their best there, and I can report to you without reservation that they are splendid in every way. It was my constant effort to preserve them and end this savage conflict honorably and with the least loss of time and a minimum sacrifice of life. Its growing bloodshed has caused me the deepest anguish and anxiety. Those gallant men will remain often in my thoughts and in my prayers always.

I am closing my 52 years of military service. When I joined the army, even before the turn of the century, it was the fulfillment of all my boyish hopes and dreams. The world has turned over many times since I took the oath at West Point, and the hopes and dreams have all since vanished, but I still remember

In his farewell address before a joint session of Congress in 1951, General Douglas MacArthur made an emotional appeal for the sympathy and support of the nation.

the refrain of one of the most popular barracks ballads of that day which proclaimed most proudly that old soldiers never die; they just fade away. And, like the old soldier of that ballad, I now close my military career and just fade away, an old soldier who tried to do his duty as God gave him the light to see that duty. Good-bye.

Not only MacArthur's text but also his performance drew wide public attention and commentary. One critic, Quincy Howe, a communications professor at the University of Illinois, paid tribute to MacArthur's ability to sustain the emotional response of his audience, a quality that all successful speakers (and actors) must master.

CONTROLLED EMOTION

If the subject you are writing or speaking about is an emotionally charged issue, you should discuss it with controlled emotion in order to get the desired response from reader or listener. An argument that becomes "hot" with emotion can easily deflect attention away from the point of view expressed to the person expressing it.

A good example of controlled emotion is the "Firing Line" debate between civil libertarian and feminist advocate Harriet Pilpel and Alan Sears, who served as executive director of the Commission on Pornography authorized by the U.S. Justice Department. Both lawyers, the participants debated the issue "Pornography and the State" on July 9, 1986, shortly after the pornography commission had published a report.*

---

*The Final Report of the Attorney General's Commission on Pornography, Washington, D.C.: U.S. Government Printing Office, 1986.

In the following excerpts Ms. Pilpel explains why she was highly critical of the report, and Sears defends it. Any discussion of a sexual issue can be highly emotional, but both of these participants remained "cool under fire" in attempts to make their arguments clear and to win the audience to their point of view.

MS. PILPEL: This commission, admittedly, in its own introduction, conducted no investigations, no studies. Their list of witnesses was hand-picked, highly in favor of people who believe that pornography as well as obscenity should be punished. Something like 160 out of 220 of the witnesses were on the side that Mr. Sears is expressing here today. When he talks about what has been happening since 1970, he makes it sound as if it is unique to this country. The sexual revolution, so called, is not unique to the United States, it is unique to the whole world.

As far as his statement that there has been under-enforcement, I don't know how many people—in the absence of proof that obscenity or pornography does any harm—would prefer their policemen to be prowling around trying to find obscene books or magazines, especially since now they are not to look for them unless they have pictures in them, would prefer their policemen to be doing that rather than detecting unlawful conduct, crimes of all kinds, including sex crimes and so forth.

Here is how Sears responded to the charge that there was no documentation that reading or viewing pornography or obscene matter can be harmful:

SEARS: Among the effects that were demonstrated by the limited social science work [highlighted in the

Commission's report] . . . we found that there was evidence of aggressive behavior toward women being increased, a feeling that there should be less punishment for rapists and other sexual offenders, that there was a greater acceptance of rape, a greater acceptance of sexual violence against women and children, a greater acceptance of the view that victims are worthless, that it was the victim's fault that they got in trouble in the first place.

[He concluded by saying] I agree . . . that there are many things that are negative [not valid in the Commission's report] but the key thing to remember is that this stuff [pornography] just has no value. The Supreme Court made that conclusion, also that it can be regulated by the state. It is demonstrably harmful.

EMOTIONS AND POINTS OF VIEW

If you were to read the full text of this debate, your opinion might or might not be changed, depending on your point of view when you first began reading it. If you had a strong opinion about the evils of pornography and its harmful effects on old and young alike, you would agree strongly with Sears's conclusions. If you had a strong opinion about the rights of a free press and other communications media, you might agree with Pilpel that suppression of pornography or whatever is purported to be pornographic is an infringement of the rights of citizens under the U.S. Constitution. However, if you had no strong opinion when you began reading the text of the debate, you could be influenced by the arguments of either Sears or Pilpel. This might help you make up your mind on where you stand in regard to pornography.

The same would be true of any emotional issue

A confrontation between opponents and supporters of abortion. In emotionally charged debates, it's often difficult to stick to facts and logic.

raised. When you are discussing an emotional issue in an essay, research paper, speech, or debate, you will be using your skills to win the approval of reader or listener to your point of view through language, narrative accounts of personal experiences, and the emotional / where you think it appropriate. When combined with the skillful use of facts and logic, appeals to the emotions can help you in your efforts to persuade.

HUMOR AS WEAPON AND REINFORCEMENT

6

When most people think of humor, they think of something that makes them smile or laugh. Humor is certainly that; but when humor is used in writing or speaking to score a point, it is much more than an attempt to get a laugh. Humor can be a formidable weapon as a means of ridiculing a person or group that holds an opposing point of view. You can also use humor to reinforce your ideas, points of view, and conclusions. When reader or audience smiles or laughs in response to a humorous phrase, statement, or story, you have achieved your goal. That smile or laugh encourages the reader or audience to agree with you on the point you are trying to make.

Humor wears many faces—wit, satire, parody, as well as the comic in situations in which there seems to be no other purpose than to reveal the ridiculous side of human nature. Yet even in situations that seem to be just plain funny there is a point being made if you look closely enough.

HUMOR AS STYLE OR APPROACH TO A SUBJECT

One of the masters of humor with a point is the syndicated newspaper columnist Art Buchwald. Many of his columns have been collected in books. They all exemplify the potential that humor offers as style or approach to a subject, when used skillfully. In a column titled "Curing a Phobia,"* he expressed the fear and frustration that millions of Americans feel toward the threat of nuclear war.

His column begins with a reference to a press conference in which General Curtis LeMay expressed the opinion that Americans seem to have a phobia about nuclear weapons. This remark led Buchwald to ponder the military attitude that nuclear bombs are just another weapon; an approach that ignored the frightening threat to human life the weapons represent. The imaginary scene Buchwald conjures up involves his visit to a crackpot psychiatrist, Dr. Adolph Strainedluff, who specializes in nuclear arms phobias. Buchwald wants to be cured of his phobia, but instead of being cured, he is castigated by the mad doctor. Here is an excerpt:

Dr. Strainedluff said, "You are a sick man. You think that just because an atomic bomb killed a few thousand people more than twenty years ago, you are threatened. You are manifesting infantile repressed hostility toward the weapons of war. In psychiatry we call this a military-industrial inferiority complex."

"I know I'm sick. You've got to help me," I begged.

---

*Art Buchwald, *The Establishment Is Alive and Well in Washington* (New York: G. P. Putnam's Sons, 1969).

Columnist Art Buchwald (mugging for the camera) makes effective use of humor in his political commentaries.

"All right. First, you haff to get over this absurd fear of nuclear bombs. You must think of them as just another weapon in our vast defensive arsenal. Ve haff bowie knives and H-bombs, and in war, one is just as good as another. You're not afraid of a knife, are you?"

"Well, I don't think about it a lot."

"So vhy should you be afraid of an H-bomb? It's another form of a knife."

"I never thought of it like that."

"Okay, so now let's look at some facts straight in the eye. In Bikini we blew up twenty bombs in an experiment. So ve thought everything would be destroyed; that's how stupid ve were. Do you know that now after all the boom-boom, the place is flourishing and the rats are fatter than they ever vas before?"

"It's good to hear."

"The coconuts are hanging from the trees, the fish are svimming in the lagoon, and the voice of the turtle can be heard in the land. The only things that don't seem to be doing so good are the land crabs."

"I don't like land crabs," I said.

"So then you don't haff anything to vorry about."

Dr. Strainedluff started playing with the hand grenade which was attached to his watch fob. "If you're going to be a happy, normal human being," he shouted, "you're going to haff to stop with all these guilty peace feelings!"

He was stomping around the room. "So get out of here with your lousy phobias and all this stuff about being afraid to die. If you're not villing to take a little fallout for the good of the country, then go back vhere you came from!"

HUMOR TO EXPRESS SKEPTICISM

Sometimes humor is used to express a skeptical point of view. This device was used by George Feifer in an article* he wrote for *Harper's* Magazine about the revolutionary changes in the Soviet Union under Gorbachev. These included *glasnost*, or "openness," the right to freely expressed opinion, and *perestroika*, the restructuring of economic and political systems more in line with the capitalist nations, though still bound to Communist party control.

To justify his skepticism, Feifer included some humorous quotes from Russian friends. One commented on the lack of public support (or trust) of the new programs, saying "the majority of people have only one concern: to avert personal disaster from another national con job. While *you* might know why we must restructure, our workers know that what counts is what you can steal *today* from your factory."

Another commented on the continuing shortage of basic necessities:

Last year only World War II veterans could buy toilet paper—yes, the old cliché about toilet paper in our land of immense forests. Now toilet paper is back, which means you find it at the end of a long line in the twentieth store you try. Yesterday I saw a distinguished-looking professor riding to work on the subway with a huge sack of his precious find. My God! I had to laugh.

---

*George Feifer, "The New God Will Fail," *Harper's* Magazine (October 1988).

HUMOR AS WEAPON AGAINST INJUSTICE

A joke or humorous story can be an effective weapon in writing or speaking against injustice. One of the women who fought long and hard to make it possible for women to vote in the United States, Susan B. Anthony, often repeated the following anecdote with good effect:

A good farmer's wife near Earlville, Illinois, who had all the rights she wanted, went to the dentist of the village, who made her a full set of false teeth, both upper and lower. The dentist pronounced them an admirable fit, but the wife declared they gave her fits to wear them; that she could neither chew nor talk with them in her mouth.

The dentist sued the husband [for slander]; his counsel brought the wife as witness; the judge ruled her off the stand, saying: "A married woman cannot be a witness in matters of joint interest between herself and her husband."

Think of it, ye good wives, the false teeth in your mouths a joint interest with your husbands, about which you are legally incompetent to speak!

HUMOR AS SOCIAL COMMENT

Humor is often used successfully as comment on social issues and attitudes. One of the most accomplished users of this technique is Russell Baker, syndicated columnist/essayist and author of many books. In an essay called "Forever Ember,"* he has

---

*Russell Baker, *The Rescue of Miss Yaskell And Other Pipe Dreams* (New York: Congdon & Weed, Inc., 1983).

fun with the popularity of self-help books, whose intent is to help people lead healthier, neurosis-free lives. His target in this essay is a book called *The Burn-Out Test*. One definition of burn-out is exhaustion, especially as the result of overwork or dissipation. Baker responds to some of the more fatuous questions posed by the book. Here are some excerpts:

I confess . . . that a few of the test's 15 questions were troubling. Oh, not question No. 1—"Do you tire more easily? Feel fatigued rather than energetic?" It is not easier for me to tire now than when I was in high school, an era when it took me a full 10 minutes after getting out of bed in the morning to become totally fatigued. In those days, of course, knowing that I had to face a Latin class at 8 a.m. was a great aid to rapid tiring. Nowadays, lacking an 8 a.m. Latin class, I am often unable to achieve deep fatigue until I have been at least 15 minutes out of the sheets.

Question No. 2—"Are people annoying you by telling you, 'You don't look so good lately.'?"—was no problem. What annoys me is people who say, "You're looking wonderful lately." In my experience you don't blurt out to somebody that he's looking wonderful unless he looks so ready for autopsy that you have to smother the impulse to ask if he has his will in order.

Question No. 5 was more troublesome. "Are you often invaded by a sadness you can't explain?" Fortunately, the temptation to answer "Yes" here was dispelled when I moved on to Question No. 8—"Are you seeing close friends and family members less frequently?"

My answer was "No, I am seeing close friends and family members as frequently as ever." And not necessarily a good thing, either, for I have noticed that these people so dear to me seem of late to be tiring more easily and feeling fatigued rather than energetic and to be working harder and harder and accomplishing less and less, thereby showing distinct symptoms of burn-out as defined by Questions No. 1 and 3.

As Baker and many other writers, speakers, and debaters have demonstrated, humor can be effective even when you are discussing a serious subject. However, humor is just one of many devices and techniques available to you. When you make use of it, make sure you are using it not as humor for its own sake but as an effective means of making a point.

RESEARCHING, OUTLINING, AND WRITING:
Blending the Elements to Make Your Point

7

There are three basic steps involved in any writing project:

1. Doing research to gather facts, comment, and other information you will need to be persuasive in making your point.
2. Making an outline, showing a logical progression of the ideas, examples, and arguments you will be using.
3. Writing: first the rough draft and then the final revisions.

Your primary sources for research are your school and local libraries. There you will find books and magazines that will provide the material you need. You may also want to make use of any tapes or video cassette recordings that have a direct bearing on the topic you will be writing about, taking notes as you listen and/or watch. Another source, depending on your subject, would be interviews with family, friends, and local experts or people with experiences that relate directly to your subject. When you have gathered all the material you need, the next step is to organize it into an outline. This is a crucial step, because unless you have a carefully constructed outline you may fail in your efforts to make your point.

SKILLFUL USE OF OUTLINE

Put in its simplest terms, an outline should have a beginning, a middle, and an end. How detailed the outline will be will depend on the material you have gathered through class notes and/or research or both, depending on the assignment. The same basic principles and techniques in outlining apply, whether it's an essay, report, research paper, speech, or notes for a debate. When you are putting an outline together, you are assembling the facts, logic, and arguments that are needed to reinforce and strengthen your point of view.

You will want to make a strong beginning with assertions and arguments that command attention. You will want to expand the arguments with facts, comments, examples, and other supporting material. You will want to close with as much strength as you began, reasserting your point of view and leaving no doubt in the reader's or hearer's mind that you have made your point.

Basically, there are three types of outline. In the *topic* outline a series of phrases are used to show how you plan to develop your ideas and arguments. The *paragraph* outline consists of sentences that indicate the thoughts, ideas, and situations you have selected for successive paragraphs. A variation of this is the *sentence* outline in which complete sentences are used for both major and supporting ideas.

This is the most comprehensive type of outline and is often used in planning long papers (or speeches and debates).

OUTLINING A RESEARCH PAPER

Suppose you were asked to write a research paper for your U.S. History class. You are given some leeway because your instructor allows you to select a topic that interests you, within the period of history covered in class and subject to his or her approval. You are expected to spend quite a bit of time on the project in study, research, and note taking. Your instructor wants the final paper to consist of seven to ten typewritten pages—in addition to title page, table of contents, illustrations, bibliography, and endnotes.

Before you begin the project, your instructor asks you to submit a tentative bibliography with at least five sources that you will be using for research. She will be following your progress throughout the project, which will cover a period of approximately two months. You will be expected to use 3" x 5" cards for research notes. These will be due for inspection at the end of the first month. A week later you will be asked to submit your outline; three weeks later your rough draft is due. All of these steps are designed to assist you in your efforts to submit the best possible paper.

Now for the hypothetical project. Let's assume you have selected the following topic: "Social Programs in the Roosevelt Years." Your aim is to identify and discuss the programs and goals that exemplify the broad concept of Roosevelt's political philosophy. Assuming you have already found and made use of research sources and have ample notes, here is how you might draft an outline for this research paper. Because it is a long paper, you decide to use the sentence outline technique, putting both major and supporting ideas into complete sentences.

SOCIAL PROGRAMS IN THE ROOSEVELT YEARS

I President Roosevelt's achievements as a social and political reformer have earned him a permanent place in history.
   A. Many of his reforms were a direct response to the national crisis created by the Depression.
   B. Congress at first was willing to enact reforms as the best solution to pressing problems.
   C. Eventually the opposition made itself heard.

II Government agencies were set up to reorganize industry and agriculture under controls.
   A. The goal was to revive the economy by spending huge amounts of public money as a "pump priming" concept.
   B. Examples include the National Recovery Administration, the Agricultural Adjustment Administration, and the Public Works Administration.
   C. Public and political reactions to these programs produced extremist points of view.

III Some of Roosevelt's programs challenged private industry and were considered threatening to the democratic concept of capitalism.

    A. Among the most controversial programs were the Tennessee Valley Authority and the Rural Electrification Administration.
    B. Many ideological battles were waged in Congress and the press over these programs.
IV Two programs that rank among the highest of Roosevelt's achievements are Social Security and the Securities and Exchange Commission.
    A. The Social Security program has saved millions of citizens from poverty and despair.
    B. The Securities and Exchange Commission is an economic safeguard.
V President Roosevelt was courageous in promoting radical programs that met the nation's needs.
    A. His critics have been unfair.
    B. He was one of America's most effective and innovative leaders.

WRITING AND REVISING:
QUESTIONS TO ASK YOURSELF

Once you have finished the first draft of your research paper, one important question in your mind will be whether it has met the length requirement. In the foregoing example it was seven to ten pages, which gives the writer quite a bit of leeway. If your paper is too long, you will need to eliminate some of the material. This should consist of the less important ideas, facts, quoted material, etc. if you need to write more, this means more research is needed. However, don't do it in a haphazard way. Study your first draft and decide where some of the sections need strengthening, then find the information, comments, or examples you need.

When your draft meets the required length, and before you begin revising it, ask yourself if you have included all the points you need to be persuasive. Secondly, ask yourself if your ideas are in the best possible order.

As you begin revising your paper, there are two key questions to ask yourself: (1) Have you expressed your thoughts clearly and precisely? (2) Are your sentences varied enough in length and structure so as to make the paper interesting to read? You will also be checking to make sure your words are spelled correctly and that your grammar is correct.

BLENDING THE ELEMENTS

To be successful, no matter what you're writing, you must blend the essential elements in a forceful, positive way that leaves no doubt about the point you're trying to make. Whether the reader or audience agrees with your point of view or not, you will win respect (and a higher grade) if your effort reflects careful research, logical reasoning, and ideas and arguments that are interesting and interestingly expressed.

Let's take the Roosevelt research paper as an example. As shown in the outline, if you had this assignment you would have a wealth of facts to use in making your point because the Roosevelt administration was the longest (1932-45) and one of the most eventful in this nation's history. The logic of your arguments could be backed up by the authorities you select to reinforce your point of view.

In appealing to the emotions, you could describe

the pathetic economic conditions that resulted from the Great Depression and the urgent need to bring relief to both workers and industry. An especially potent emotional issue would be the Social Security program. You could devote one or more paragraphs to the plight of many of the nation's elderly who were living in poverty at that time. There is also the sad plight of the farmers, many of whom lost their farms when extreme drought ruined their crops. There would be many other examples.

If you wanted to inject some humor into the paper, you could cite some of the comic sketches by comedians and writers who were either pro- or anti-Roosevelt, such as Fred Allen, Robert Benchley, James Thurber and others. You might want to use some of the famous cartoons of the period as illustrations, including those from the *New Yorker* Magazine and other periodicals. Admittedly, the Roosevelt era is rich in all kinds of material for research, but the same approach can be used whatever the subject of your research paper, speech, or debate. Research will point the way.

Your challenge will be the same: to be persuasive in making your point. All of the elements will be there—facts, logic, language, emotion, humor—waiting for you to put them to good use. Any project takes time, study, organization, and care in the thinking and writing. But if you put forth the needed effort, you can be successful in making your point and at the same time learn a useful skill: how to be persuasive.

APPENDIX A: CHOOSING A TOPIC

There will be times when your instructor will allow you the freedom of choosing a topic for an essay, report, research paper, or speech. You may be given a list of topics to choose from, or you may be left entirely on your own. When this happens, you should either (1) select a topic in which you already have some knowledge or experience or (2) choose a topic that is unfamiliar but one in which you have a strong interest.

Interest should be your guide, because if you're interested in a subject, you will give it the thought and study needed to make your written material both interesting and persuasive. Armed with a strong interest in a subject, you will soon discover the interest growing as you learn more about it and begin putting notes down on paper.

BECOMING INVOLVED

It will help your writing and your powers of persuasion if your topic is one that matters to you deeply. In this way you become personally involved in what you're writing about and will put forth the effort needed to successfully make your point.

Before you begin the research, you may already have a strong opinion about a particular issue, attitude, or philosophy, but without facts and logical arguments, you can't convince others that you know what you are writing or speaking about.

The more controversial the issue, the stronger your arguments need to be. Whatever topic you choose to write about, however, you need to be able to discuss it knowledgeably, logically, and persuasively. Once you have the topic in mind, make notes about what you know about it and how you feel about it. Think of personal experiences that you, your friends, or family have had that relate directly to your topic. Talk to them about it. You can do this before you start the research as well as while your research is progressing.

This will help to clarify your point of view and may result in some good ideas for you to act on. For example, suppose you are going to write a paper on "Parents—What a Child Owes Her Parents—What Parents Owe Their Children." Talking with friends and family about this concern will provide interesting and convincing material for your paper. If some of your points of view are controversial, you might suddenly have a wealth of supporting arguments to use, all based on the personal experiences of those you interviewed. Armed with enough facts and logical arguments, you could be very successful indeed in making your point.

BEFORE YOU BEGIN

Before you begin working on your paper, however, you should have a clear idea of what your purpose is.

If your subject is parent-child relationships, is your purpose to convince the reader that certain attitudes on the part of children or parents are wrong? Then you should make a strong case for changing those attitudes.

KEEP READER OR AUDIENCE IN MIND

You should also be conscious of the reader or audience for which your paper is intended. Will you be writing with your friends and other students in mind, or will your point of view be directed at parents? You should decide this before you start your research.

Once you have gathered sufficient information and ideas from your research, the next step is to organize the material in a logical way, noting where your arguments need strengthening in order to make your point clearly and emphatically. Then begin the writing.

A NOTE ABOUT "TONE"

You should be concerned about the tone reflected in your paper. If you get too emotional in your arguments, you may develop an angry, accusative, or complaining tone that will detract from your arguments. Your tone should be calm and reasonable, reflecting an attitude based on facts and logical arguments presented in support of your point of view.

APPENDIX B:
Topics for Essays, Reports, Research Papers, Speeches, and Debates

The following list of topics is offered as a starting point in deciding what topic and what point of view best fits your interest. Many of these topics have special relevance to anyone living in the closing years of the twentieth century. Others are topics that continue to have universal interest because they represent basic concerns of human beings. Some points of view are suggested; however, your approach to a particular topic will depend on your own point of view and the arguments you can muster in making your point.

ESSAYS, REPORTS, RESEARCH PAPERS

Basic Needs
Friendship
Love
Security—Personal and Economic

Crime
Dealing with Criminals—Sentencing and Rehabilitation

Environmental Concerns
Acid Rain
Air Pollution
Toxic Waste
Water Pollution

Family Concerns, Family Relationships
Adoption
Aging—Respect for and Care of the Elderly
Battered Wives, Mothers, and Children
Fathers and Sons—What's a good relationship? What's a bad or problem-causing relationship?
Mothers and Daughters—What's a good relationship? What's a bad or problem-causing relationship?
Single Mothers

Financial Concerns
Learning How to Handle Money—Personal Finances
Success—What It Means to Be Financially Successful

Health and Public Safety
Alcohol Abuse
Drug Abuse
Tobacco Use

Personal Concerns, Personal Relationships
Being Yourself—Why a Person Should Be Himself/Herself and Not Pretend or Aspire to Be Someone Else

Beauty—What It Is—Physical Beauty—Spiritual Beauty—How to Be a Beautiful Person
Grief—How to Accept Death When Someone Close to You Dies

Poverty
The Black Underclass—Is there any hope for this group? What is the government doing about it? What are blacks doing to help blacks?

Prejudice
Anti-Semitism
Bigotry—racial and religious hatred
The Horrors of the Holocaust—The Ultimate Evil of Prejudice
The Ku Klux Klan

Politics
Communism
Conservatism—What a Conservative Is
Democracy
Freedom of Speech—What does it mean? What should it mean?
Liberalism—What a Liberal Is
Fascism—What a Fascist Is
Patriotism
Totalitarianism

Sexual Concerns and Relationships
Birth Control—How soon should minors become knowledgeable?
Dating
Going Steady
Teenage Pregnancy

War and Other Military Concerns
Vietnam War—Why It Was an Unpopular War

Miscellaneous
Artificial Intelligence
Choosing A Profession—Why I Want to Be (You Name It)
Why I Like to Gamble
What I Would Do If I Won the State Lottery

SPEECHES

Basic Needs
The Good Life—What is it?

Crime
How Can We Deter Crime?

Environmental Concerns
The Greenhouse Effect is already here.

Family Concerns,
Family Relationships
Problem Children—Why problems develop and how they should be handled.

Health and Public Safety
Steroids—The Medical and Moral Consequences

Personal Concerns,
Personal Relationships
Dieting—Do special diets really work? Are they good for your health? Who should diet?
"Recreational" Drugs—The Dangers and the Consequences

Poverty
The Homeless—A National Shame—What Should Be Done

Prejudice
American Indians—How They Have Been Hurt by Prejudice.
Apartheid in the Republic of South Africa—The Evils It Has Produced

Politics
Ethics in Politics and Government
U.S.-Soviet Relations
U.S.-China Relations

*Sexual Concerns
   and Relationships*
Bachelors and Single Women—Why They Stay Single So Long Today
Homosexuality—Gay Rights—Have attitudes about sexual orientation changed?
Right to Life (Anti-abortion Stand)
Sex and Responsibility
Woman's Choice (Right to Abortion)

*War and Other
   Military Concerns*
Arms Control—Nuclear and Conventional Arms—Reducing Military Power and Threats

Miscellaneous
Astrology—Reading the Future in the Stars—A harmless hoax or has it proven to have any validity? Why President Reagan's Wife Consulted an Astrologer and the Results
Television—When It's a Blessing, When It's a Curse
The Twenty-First Century—How Life Will Be Different—What Things Won't Happen—What I Would Like to Have Happen

DEBATES

Crime
Do we need more prison cells or better methods of rehabilitation?

Environmental Concerns
Rain Forests—Why They Should Be Protected from Development

Family Concerns, Family Relationships
Day Care—Positive and Negative Aspects
Parents—What a Child Owes His Parents—What Parents Owe Their Children

Financial Concerns
The National Debt—What We Should Do About It

Health and Public Safety
Why I Do (Do Not) Believe in Gun Control

Personal Concerns, Personal Relationships
Heredity vs. Environment—Which is more important in influencing a person's likes, dislikes, character?
Marriage Contracts—Are They a Good Idea or a Bad Idea?

Poverty
The Poor—How They Can Be Helped Out of Poverty—Why They Are Poor and Can't Help Themselves

Prejudice
Neo-Nazis and Other Hate Groups—Should They Be Allowed to Exist?

Politics
Censorship of High School Newspapers—Pro or Con
Israel vs. the Arabs—Is Israel preventing peace in the Middle East?
United Nations—Is It Worth the Investment?

Sexual Concerns and Relationships
Abortion Clinics—Should they be tax supported?
AIDS Testing—Who Should Be Tested and Why—The Problem of Confidentiality
Living Together vs. Marriage—Pro or Con
Sex—Abstinence vs. Promiscuity

War and Other Military Concerns
Nuclear Weapons—Why They Should (Should Not) Be Banned

FOR FURTHER READING

Andersen, Martin P., Wesley Lewis, and James Murray. *The Speaker And His Audience.* New York: Harper & Row, 1964.

Arnold, Carroll C., Douglas Ehninger, and John C. Gerber. *The Speaker's Resource Book.* Chicago: Scott, Foresman and Company, 1961.

Barzun, Jacques. *Simple & Direct, A Rhetoric for Writers,* New York: Harper & Row, 1975.

Carney, James D., and Richard K. Scheer. *Fundamentals of Logic.* New York: Macmillan Publishing Co., 1974.

Dunbar, Robert E. *How to Debate.* New York: Franklin Watts, 1987.

Foerster, Norman, and J. M. Steadman, Jr. *Writing*

and Thinking, Boston: Houghton Mifflin Company, 1941.

Minnick, Wayne C. *The Art of Persuasion*, Boston: Houghton Mifflin Company, 1968.

Orwell, George. *On Shooting An Elephant, and Other Essays.* New York: Harcourt, Brace & World, Inc., 1950.

Scott, Robert L., and Douglas W. Ehninger. *The Speaker's Reader: Concepts in Communication.* Chicago: Scott Foresman and Company, 1969.

Stevenson, Marjolyn. *English Syntax.* Boston: Little, Brown and Company, 1987.

Strunk, William, Jr., and E. B. White. *Elements of Style.* New York: Macmillan Publishing Co., 1979.

INDEX

Abolition movement, 15–16, 64–65
Active voice, use of, 49–50
Advertising, 18–19
American Heritage Dictionary, 51
American Medical Association, 57
Anthony, Susan B., 31–33, 81

Baker, Russell, 81–83
"Ban Boxing" editorial, 22–23
Bibliography for research paper, 86
Boxing, 22–23
Buchwald, Art, 77–79

Catcher in the Rye (Salinger), 37
Circular reasoning, 35
Civil disobedience, 65–68
"Civil Disobedience" (Thoreau), 65–67
Civil rights movement, 12–15, 68
Clichés, use of, 53
Commission on Pornography, 71
Conciseness, 46–49
Conrad, John P., 38
Crimean War, 24–28
"Curing a Phobia" (Buchwald), 77–79

Debating, 11

Declaration of Independence, 15
Deduction, unwarranted, 35–37
Deductive reasoning, 30–33
Dictionary, use of, 51
Directness, importance of, 58–59
Douglas, Stephen A., 16
Dunbar, Robert E., 60

Elements of Style (Strunk and White), 46
Elvridge, Ford, 57
Emotions, appealing to, 63–75, 89–90

Facts, use of, 21–29, 89
False assumptions, 35
Feifer, George, 80
Figures of speech, 52–53
"Firing Line" debates:
July 1986, 71
May 1987, 37–39
Foerster, Norman, 42
"Forever Ember" (Baker), 81–83
"Four Freedoms" (Roosevelt), 44

Gandhi, Mahatma, 67–68
Generalization, 35

Glasnost, 80
Gorbachev, Mikhail, 80

Harper's, 80
How to Debate, 60
Howe, Quincy, 71
Humor, use of, 76–83, 90
Hyperbole, 53

"I Have a Dream" (King), 12–14
Illogical thinking, 34–39
Inductive reasoning, 33–34
Injustice and humor, 81
Interviewing, 85

Jargon, use of, 53
Jefferson, Thomas, 15

Kennedy, John F., 16–18
Keller, Helen, 35
King, Martin Luther, Jr., 12–15, 68
Korean War, 68

Language, use of, 42–62
LeMay, Curtis, 77
Library, use of, 84
Lincoln, Abraham, 16
Lincoln-Douglas debate, 16
Logic, use of, 30–41, 89

MacArthur, Douglas, 68–71
Malapropisms, 52
March on Washington (August 1963), 12
Martin Luther King Day, 15
Metaphors, 52–53

Narrative technique, 64
NATO, 38–39
New Republic, The, 22
Nightingale, Florence, 24–28
Non-Violent Resistance (Gandhi), 68
Nuclear war, 77–79

Ohio State University, 57
Orwell, George, 55
Outlining, 84, 85–88
Out-of-context quotations, 28–29

Paragraph outline, 85
Peace Corps, 18
Perestroika, 80
Persuasion, power of, 11–20
Pilpel, Harriet, 71–72
Politics and the English Language (Orwell), 55
Pornography, 71–73
"Pornography and the State" debate, 71
Precise language, choice of, 50–52
Psychosomatic illness, 57–58
Public speaking, 11

Quoted material, 28–29, 37

Research, 21–22, 84–85, 90
Revising, 88–89
Right to vote, 31–33, 81
Roget's Thesaurus, 51
Roosevelt, Franklin D., 44, 86, 87
Satyagraha, 67–68
Schindler, John, 57–58
Sears, Alan, 71–73
Self-contradiction, 34–35
Self-help books, 82–83
Sentence outline, 85–86
Sentence structure, 59–61
Simile, 53
Simplicity, importance of, 58–59
Skepticism and humor, 80
Slang, use of, 53
Slavery, 15–16, 64–65
Social comment and humor, 81–83

Sockman, Ralph, 56–57
Steadman, J. M., Jr., 42
Stevenson, Robert Louis, 35
Stillwell, Henry, 37
Strunk, William, Jr., 46

Thoreau, Henry David, 65–67
Topic, choice of, 91–101
Topic outline, 85
Truman, Harry S., 68
Tyson, Mike, 22

United Nations, 38–39

Van Den Haag, Ernest, 38
Vidal, Gore, 53

Walden (Thoreau), 65
Walters, Vernon, 38–39
White, E. B., 46, 55
Women's suffrage, 31–33, 81
Words, sound of, 61–62
Writing, 55–56, 84, 88–90
Writing and Thinking (Foerster and Steadman), 42

ABOUT THE AUTHOR

Robert E. Dunbar is a free-lance writer who lives in Damariscotta, Maine. His two previous books for Franklin Watts were *The Heart and Circulatory System* and *How to Debate.*

	DATE DUE		

5010

808
DUN

Dunbar, Robert E.

Making your point : how to speak and write persuasively.

LIBERTY HIGH SCHOOL

382249 01390   04382C   86